LIFE IN COMMUNITY

LIFE IN COMMUNITY

An illustrated and abridged edition of Jean Vanier's classic

COMMUNITY AND GROWTH

DARTON·LONGMAN+TODD

First published in English in 2019 by
Darton, Longman and Todd Ltd
1 Spencer Court
140 – 142 Wandsworth High Street
London SW18 4JJ

Text © 2019 Jean Vanier
Illustrations © Seán O'Brien

With thanks to Isabelle Aumont, Chris Asprey, Heather Coogan and Amy Merone.

Published under licence from Mame, Paris, publisher of the first edition in French,
La Communauté, (2017).

ISBN: 978-0-232-53398-9

Designed and produced by Judy Linard.
Printed and bound by Imak Offset.

CONTENTS

INTRODUCTION

a few days ago, a young man asked me what a community is. When I responded by asking him, 'What do you think?' he said, 'It's a group of men and women who are closed in on themselves.' No, it's precisely the opposite. To be closed is what a sect is, but not a community. A community is a group of men and women who love and respect one another, and genuinely look out for each other. They meet or live together for the sake of a common, God-given mission. That mission can be very varied: welcoming those in difficulty in Jesus' name, working for peace in situations of grave unrest, living a life of prayer and contemplation for the sake of the world, being a sign in society that people of difference can live joyfully together, uniting and working together for the sake of the planet, etc.

* * *

At first sight, community life seems wonderful: a true ideal. But let's admit it: it's not easy to live alongside people who are very different than ourselves. I myself have been living in a L'Arche Community for more than fifty years. Our aim is to live together: people with intellectual disabilities and others who come to be with them. Each member of a community has their own temperament, their weaknesses, their faults, their wounds, their story, their defence mechanisms, often as a consequence of childhood experience. People of different ages, cultures, religions, abilities or disabilities, live together, each one with their own story. So it is not always easy to live and work together, while loving and respecting one another, and truly listening to each other.

Everyone in the community may well have good intentions. However, even if each person has freely chosen to be there, and wants to live the life of the community, nevertheless we are all unique, and are capable of loving and welcoming others only in our own individual way, and to a greater or lesser extent. In every person, there is a gap between the desire to love and accept everyone else, and the reality of loving them as a brother or a sister in everyday life. So the community is not an ideal, where each person is discovered to be perfect; for we are all human beings, and each of us has our weaknesses and difficulties in opening ourselves up to others in relationship. And so community becomes a place of healing and liberating our hearts, a place where we gradually learn to love and forgive one another from day to day. In community life, there are always times of conflict and difficulties in relationship. That is why a community is a place of belonging for the sake of becoming. We belong to each other for the sake of a mission: in order that each of us would become freer, happier, more deeply human, more mature, more responsible, more capable of loving and accepting those who are different to us. In other words, living together is a journey on which each person agrees to resist closing in on themselves, on their own ego, in order to be more open to others. That implies a sort of conversion, a change of values, a transformed life that is open to God and to God's love. And that conversion or transformation does not happen once and for all, it needs to happen again and again each day, through prayer and individual effort. It involves a daily struggle against egocentric impulses, which are caused and perpetuated by tiredness and failures of various kinds, which can occur at any moment. That is why each person needs the strength that comes from the heart of Jesus, in order to continue the journey towards transformation.

* * *

It must be admitted that we live in a society where children are very quickly pushed by their school towards achieving things as individuals. They need to get good marks, to be winners on the sports field, to appear to be the best at many things, to be appreciated and recognised by parents and teachers alike. And not to succeed is to risk being punished. So many people in our society find themselves in a perpetual battle to succeed, to get a good job, to get promoted, to receive honours and recognition. We live in a competitive world. There are also people who, because of health problems, education, their family or social background, do not succeed to the same degree. They feel humiliated, are considered inferior, and harbour in their hearts a great deal of anger, and sometimes anguish.

An individual or individualistic mind-set, the need to appear better than everyone else, according to the values of one's family or society – all that is opposed to the way of life in community, where what is needed is openness to others, and values such as love, service and hospitality towards those who are different. Indeed, constantly focusing on ourselves or on our own group puts strain on our relationships with other people, and sometimes on relations between different groups; and this strain leads to fear, violence, hatred and various forms of war. That is how terrible rifts and splits open up in society, between individuals and social, political or religious groups.

* * *

Certain communities carry out a genuine peace mission, by seeking to tear down the walls that separate people and groups from each other. The perspectives that underpin these communities are based in the conviction that each person is precious, wherever he or she is from, and belongs to the great human family spread throughout the world. Each person is a child of God.

* * *

In his book on Pope Francis, André Ricardi says that every community is founded on a story and on a hope for some kind of utopia. This utopia is the dream of a world that might be possible, where everyone loves each other, and where there is no hatred or fear. This utopian hope for peace in the world is at the heart of every community. In creating the universe, didn't God want all human beings to be united? L'Arche's mission is undoubtedly to assist and welcome people with learning disabilities, to help them live a better life. But beyond that mission lies a utopia: that every man and woman throughout the world would become more fully human – happier, more mature, more loving.

* * *

It takes time time – a whole lifetime, in fact – for each member of the community to move away from an egocentric perspective and open up to others, to become a brother or sister to all. It takes God's strength, spirituality, and daily nourishment, to have the energy needed to work for true community and for its mission. Indeed, everyone in community can easily fall prey to tiredness, discouragement, even depression, causing them to close in on themselves. Each one of us needs to take care of ourselves, our health and well-being, to get enough rest, to receive the spiritual nourishment we need to sustain our motivation to love. That is also true for the community as a whole, if it is to grow in faithfulness to its mission.

In the 1960s and 1970s the time was ripe for starting new communities. Many people wanted to oppose various forms of heavy-handed authoritarianism in Church and society, in institutions and corporations, and were looking for a new approach. So, in May 1968, people were crying out for a new democratic society. Many people also wanted, idealistically, to live in community, without realising the difficulties entailed in that way of life. A good number of these idealistic communities quickly died. L'Arche managed to survive during those years, because the mission to live with people who had been excluded and marginalised helped to strengthen our life in community.

Today, people are crying out again for community life, because so many of the younger generation are starting to become disillusioned with individualism and with a form of personal freedom that separates us from each other. They find themselves trapped in the anguish of loneliness. People are also becoming aware that the major crisis facing humankind today lies in the terrible separation, and the shocking gap, that exists between the wealthy and well-off, and those who live in poverty and deprivation.

* * *

This book is intended to offer some of the ingredients necessary for living a genuine community life, that feast of brotherly and sisterly love, where people of difference encounter each other and are transformed. Community attempts to combine growth towards personal freedom with shared life, in a space where everyone receives the security, mutual support and friendship they need. Thus, a new vision is emerging, where community life, notwithstanding all its difficulties, is the path of hope we need for transforming hearts and creating a more peaceful world.

The chapters in this book first appeared in a complete edition of the book *Community and Growth*, first published by DLT in 1979. This work is a new edition of extracts from that book, alongside artwork by Seán O'Brien, who is a professional illustrator. Each illustration depicts in the form of an image the content of the text next to it. The book was inspired by a group of friends from two organisations, APA (Association pour l'amitié – Association of Friends) and Lazare, which are communities where homeless men and women live alongside volunteers. They wanted members of their communities, many of whom respond more readily to expressive images than to written texts, to be able to use my book as a training tool for community life. L'Arche Communities, which also welcome many people who are unable to read, were obviously part of this initiative as well.

JEAN VANIER

THE CALL

The Foundations of Community

Life in community is painful, but it is also a marvellous adventure and a source of life.

THE ADVENTURE OF LIFE IN COMMUNITY

This book tries to clarify the conditions which are necessary to life in community. It is no thesis or treatise. It is made up of a series of starting-points for reflection, which I have discovered not through books, but through everyday life, through my mistakes, my set-backs and my personal failings, through the inspiration of God and my brothers and sisters, and through the moments of unity between us as well as the tension and suffering. Life in community is painful but it is also a marvellous adventure and a source of life. My hope is that many people can live this adventure, which in the end is one of inner liberation – the freedom to love and to be loved.

As the Father has loved me, so have I loved you; abide in my love. This is my commandment, that you love one another as I have loved you. Greater love has no man than this, that a man lay down his life for his friends. (John 15:9, 12 – 13)

They keep a foot in each camp and live a compromise,
without finding their real identity.

THE CALL

This call is an invitation: 'Come with me.' It is an invitation not primarily to generosity, but to a meeting in love. Then the person meets others who are called and they begin to live community.

To enter into a new covenant and belong to a new people, a community with new values, we have to leave another people – those with whom we have lived – with other values and other norms: wealth, possessions, social prestige, revolution, drugs, delinquency, whatever. This passage from one people to another can be a very painful uprooting, and usually takes time. Many do not achieve it, because they do not want to choose or to cut themselves off from their old life. They keep a foot in each camp and live a compromise, without finding their real identity.

To follow the call to live in a community, you have to be able to choose. The fundamental experience is a gift of God, which sometimes comes as a surprise. But this experience is fragile, like a little seed planted in the ground. After the initial experience, you have to know how to take its consequences and eliminate certain values to adopt new ones. So, gradually, comes the orientation towards a positive and definitive choice for community.

Inner growth is only possible when we commit
ourselves with and to others.

FREEDOM AND COMMITMENT

So in community everything starts with this recognition of being in communion one with another; we are made to be together. You wake up one morning knowing that the bonds have been woven; and then you make the active decision to commit yourself and promise faithfulness, which the community must confirm.

Some people flee from commitment because they are frightened that if they put down roots in one soil they will curtail their freedom and never be able to look elsewhere. It is true that if you marry one woman you give up millions of others – and that's a curtailment of freedom! But freedom doesn't grow in the abstract; it grows in a particular soil with particular people. Inner growth is only possible when we commit ourselves with and to others. We all have to pass through a certain death and time of grief when we make choices and become rooted. We mourn what we have left behind.

We want to belong to a group, but at the same time ...

THE RISK OF LOVING

Each person with his or her history of being accepted or rejected, with his or her past history of inner pain and difficulties in relationships with parents, is different. In each one there is a yearning for community and belonging, but at the same time a fear of it. Love is what we most want, yet it is what we fear the most. Love makes us vulnerable and open, but then we can be hurt through rejection and separation. We may crave for love, but then be frightened of losing our liberty and creativity. We want to belong to a group, but we fear a certain death in the group because we may not be seen as unique. We want love, but fear the dependence and commitment it implies; we fear being used, manipulated, smothered and spoiled. We are all so ambivalent toward love, communion and belonging.

If community is belonging and openness, it is also
loving concern for each person.

COMMUNITY: A PLACE OF CARING

*I*f community is belonging and openness, it is also loving concern for each person. In other words we could say it is caring, bonding and mission. Three elements define it.

In community people care for each other and not just for the community in the abstract, as a whole, as an institution or as an ideal way of life. It is people that matter; to love and care for the people that are there, just as they are. It is to care for them in such a way that they may grow according to the plan of God and thus give much life. And it is not just caring in a passing way, but in a permanent way. Because people are bonded one to another, they make up one family, one people, one flock. And this people has been called together to be a sign and a witness, to accomplish a particular mission which is their charism, their gift.

The difference between community and a group of friends is that in a community we verbalise our mutual belonging and bonding. We announce the goals and the spirit that unites us. We recognise together that we are responsible for one another. We recognise also that this bonding comes from God; it is a gift from God. It is he who has chosen us and called us together in a covenant of love and mutual caring.

They start lifting their masks and barriers to become vulnerable.

24

BENEATH THE MASKS

When people enter community, especially from a place of loneliness in a big city or from a place of aggression and rejection, they find the warmth and the love exhilarating. This permits them to start lifting their masks and barriers and to become vulnerable. They may enter into a time of communion and great joy.

But then too, as they lift their masks and become vulnerable, they discover that community can be a terrible place, because it is a place of relationship; it is the revelation of our wounded emotions and of how painful it can be to live with others, especially with some people. It is so much easier to live alone and just *do* things for others, when one feels like it.

Community is the place where our limitations, our fears and our egoism are revealed to us. We discover our poverty and our weaknesses, our inability to get on with some people, our mental and emotional blocks, our affective or sexual disturbances, our seemingly insatiable desires, our frustrations and jealousies, our hatred and our wish to destroy. While we are alone, we could believe we loved everyone. Now that we are with others, living with them all the time, we realise how incapable we are of loving, how much we deny to others, how closed in on ourselves we are.

Seán

Some people find it hard to live with others.

COMMUNITY:
A DIFFERENT WAY

Some people find it hard to live with others. They need a lot of time to themselves, a great sense of freedom and, above all, no tensions. They simply must not feel under pressure, for, if they do, they will become depressed or aggressive. These people are often very sensitive and delicate; they have almost too great a richness of heart. They could not cope with the difficulties of community life. They are called rather to live alone or with a few privileged friends. They must not be made to think that, because community life – in its more limited sense of living together – is not for them, they have no place, gift or vocation. Their gift is different. They are called to be witnesses to live in another way. And they can find a certain community life with friends or groups, with whom they meet regularly to pray and to share.

We choose our own friends; but in our families, we do not choose our brothers and sisters; they are given to us. So it is in community life.

28

COMMUNITY IS GIVEN TO US

We shouldn't seek the ideal community. It is a question of loving those whom God has set beside us today. They are signs of God. We might have chosen different people, people who were more cheerful and intelligent. But these are the ones God has given us, to create and live a covenant. We choose our own friends; but in our families, we do not choose our brothers and sisters; they are given to us. So it is in community life.

The greatness of humanity lies in the acceptance
of our insignificance.

EVERYDAY HEROISM

a community which is just an explosion of heroism is not a true community. True community implies a way of life, a way of living and seeing reality; it implies above all fidelity in the daily round. And this is made up of simple things – getting meals, using and washing the dishes and using them again, going to meetings – as well as gift, joy and celebration; and it is made up of forgiving seventy times seventy-seven.

A community is only being created when its members accept that they are not going to achieve great things, that they are not going to be heroes, but simply live each day with new hope, like children, in wonderment as the sun rises and in thanksgiving as it sets. Community is only being created when they have recognised that the greatness of humanity lies in the acceptance of our insignificance, our human condition and our earth, and to thank God for having put in a finite body the seeds of eternity which are visible in small and daily gestures of love and forgiveness.

The beauty of people is in their fidelity to the wonder of each day.

We are interdependent.

UNITED IN GOD'S EYES

When we know our people, we also realise that we need them, that they and we are interdependent; they open our hearts and call us to live. We are not better than they are – we are there together, for each other. We are united in the covenant which flows from the covenant between God and his people, God and the poorest.

GROWTH

Growing alone and together
through joys and difficulties

During this time of 'depression', everything becomes dark;
people now only see the faults of others and the community;
everything gets on their nerves.

FROM IDEALS
TO REALITY

*P*eople enter community to be happy. They stay when they find happiness comes in making others happy.

Almost everyone finds their early days in a community ideal. It all seems perfect. They seem unable to see the drawbacks; they only see what is good. Everything is marvellous; everything is beautiful.

And then comes the period of let-down – generally linked to a time of tiredness, a sense of loneliness or homesickness, some setback, a brush with authority. During this time of 'depression', everything becomes dark; people now see only the faults of others and the community; everything gets on their nerves.

The greater their idealisation of the community at the start, the more they put the people at its head on pedestals, the greater the disenchantment. It's from a height that you fall down into a pit. If people manage to get through this second period, they come to the third phase – that of realism and true commitment, of covenant. Members of the community are no longer saints or devils, but people – each a mixture of good and bad, each growing and each with their own hope. It is at this time of realism that people put their roots down. The community is neither heaven nor hell, but planted firmly on earth, and they are ready to walk in it and with it. They accept the other members and the community as they are; they are confident that together they can grow towards something more beautiful.

People very quickly get together with those
who are like themselves.

SURPASSING FRIENDSHIPS ...

*T*he two great dangers of community are 'friends' and 'enemies'. People very quickly get together with those who are like themselves; we all like to be with someone who pleases us, who shares our ideas, ways of looking at life and sense of humour. We nourish each other, we flatter each other: 'You are marvellous' – 'So are you' – 'We are marvellous because we are intelligent and clever.' Human friendships can very quickly become a club of mediocrities, enclosed in mutual flattery and approval, preventing people from seeing their inner poverty and wounds. Friendship is then no longer a spur to grow, to go further, to be of greater service to our brothers and sisters, to be more faithful to the gifts we have been given, more attentive to the Spirit, and to continue walking across the desert to the land of liberation. Friendship then becomes stifling, a barrier between ourselves and others and their needs. It becomes an emotional dependence which is a form of slavery.

There are also 'antipathies' in community.

... AND ENMITIES

There are also 'antipathies' in community. There are always people with whom we don't agree, who block us, who contradict us and who stifle the treasure of our life and our freedom. Their presence seems to awaken our own poverty, guilty feelings and inner wounds; it seems menacing and brings out in us either aggression or a sort of fear and servile regression. We seem incapable of expressing ourselves or even of living peacefully when we are with them. Others bring out our envy and jealousy; they are everything we wish we were ourselves. Their presence reminds us of what we are not; their radiance and their intelligence underline our own poverty. Others ask too much of us; we cannot respond to their incessant emotional demands and we have to push them away. These are the 'enemies'. They endanger us, and, even if we dare not admit it, we hate them. Certainly, this is only a psychological hatred – it isn't yet a moral hatred, because it is not deliberate. But even so, we just wish these people didn't exist! If they disappeared or died, it would seem like a liberation.

A community is only a community when most of its members have consciously decided to break these barriers and come out of their cocoons of 'friendship', to stretch out their hand to their enemies.

BUILDING COMMUNITY

These blocks, as well as affinity between different personalities, are natural. They come from an emotional immaturity and from many elements from our childhood over which we have no control. But it would be foolish to deny them.

But if we let ourselves be guided by our emotional reactions, cliques will form within the community. It will become no longer a community, a place of communion, but a collection of people more or less shut into different groups cut off from one another.

When you go into some communities, you can quickly sense these tensions and underground battles. People don't look each other in the face. They pass each other in the corridors like ships in the night. A community is only a community when most of its members have consciously decided to break these barriers and come out of their cocoons of 'friendship' to stretch out their hand to their enemies.

But the journey is a long one. A community isn't built in a day. In fact, it is never completely finished! It is always either growing towards greater love or else regressing, as people accept or refuse to descend into the tunnel of pain to be reborn in the spirit.

The friend of time doesn't spend all day saying,
'I haven't got time.'

BE PATIENT

Perhaps the essential quality for anyone who lives in community is patience: a recognition that we, others, and the whole community take time to grow. Nothing is achieved in a day. If we are to live in community, we have to be friends of time.

And the friend of time doesn't spend all day saying: 'I haven't got time.' He doesn't fight with time. He accepts it and cherishes it.

It is only when tensions come to a head like a boil that we can try to treat the infection at its roots.

TENSIONS LEAD TO GROWTH

Communities need tensions if they are to grow and deepen. Tensions come from conflicts within each person – conflicts born out of a refusal of personal and community growth, conflicts between individual egoisms, conflicts arising from a diminishing *gratuité*, from a clash of temperaments and from individual psychological difficulties. These are natural tensions.

And each of them brings the whole community, as well as each individual member of it, face to face with its own poverty, inability to cope, weariness, aggression and depression. These can be important times if we realise that the treasure of the community is in danger. When everything is going well, when the community feels it is living successfully, its members tend to let their energies dissipate, and to listen less carefully to each other. Tensions bring people back to the reality of their helplessness; obliging them to spend more time in prayer and dialogue, to work patiently to overcome the crisis and refind lost unity; making them understand that the community is more than just a human reality, that it also needs the spirit of God if it is to live and deepen. Tensions often mark the necessary step towards a greater unity as well, by revealing flaws which demand re-evaluation, reorganisation and a greater humility. Sometimes the brutal explosion of one tension simply reveals another which is latent. It is only when tensions come to a head like a boil that we can try to treat the infection at its roots.

47

The tongue is one of the smallest parts of our body,
but it can sow death.

BEING PATIENT WITH OURSELVES

*I*t is a long haul to transform our emotional make-up so that we can start really loving our enemy. We have to be patient with our feelings and fears; we have to be merciful to ourselves. If we are to make the passage to acceptance and love of the other – all the others – we must start very simply, by recognising our own blocks, jealousies, ways of comparing ourselves to others, prejudices and hatreds. We have to recognise that we are poor creatures, that we are what we are. And we have to ask our Father to forgive and purify us. It is good, then, to speak to a spiritual guide, who perhaps can help us to understand what is happening, strengthen us in our efforts and help us discover God's pardon.

Once we have recognised that a branch is twisted, that we have these blocks of antipathy, the next step is to try to be careful of how we speak. We have to try to hold our tongue, which can so quickly sow discord, which likes to spread the faults and mistakes of others, which rejoices when it can prove someone wrong. The tongue is one of the smallest parts of our body, but it can sow death. We are quick to magnify the faults of others, just to hide our own. It is so often 'they' who are wrong. When we accept our own flaws, it is easier to accept those of others.

When we accept that we have weaknesses and flaws,
we can accept the weaknesses and flaws of others.

ACCEPT AND FORGIVE

As long as we refuse to accept that we are a mixture of light and darkness, of positive qualities and failings, or love and hate, of altruism and egocentricity, of maturity and immaturity, and that we are all children of the same Father, we will continue to divide the world into enemies (the 'baddies') and friends (the 'goodies'). We will go on throwing up barriers around ourselves and our communities, spreading prejudice.

When we accept that we have weaknesses and flaws, that we have sinned against God and against our brothers and sisters, but that we are forgiven and can grow towards inner freedom and truer love, then we can accept the weaknesses and flaws of others. They too are forgiven by God and are growing towards the freedom of love. We can look at all men and women with realism and love. We can begin to see in them the wound of pain that brings up fear, but also their gift which we can love and admire.

We must learn to forgive and forgive and forgive every day, day after day.

FORGIVENESS, SEVEN TIMES SEVENTY-SEVEN

Community is the place of forgiveness. Living together implies a cross, a constant effort, an acceptance which is daily, and mutual forgiveness.

If we come into community without knowing that the reason we come is to learn to forgive and be forgiven seven times seventy-seven times, we will soon be disappointed.

But forgiveness is not simply saying to someone who has had a fit of anger, slammed the doors and behaved in an 'anti-community' way: 'I forgive you'. When people have power and are well settled in community, it is easy to 'wield' forgiveness. To forgive is also to understand the cry behind the behaviour. People are saying something through their anger and/or anti-social behaviour. Perhaps they feel rejected. Perhaps they feel that no one is listening or maybe they feel incapable of expressing what is inside them. Perhaps the community is being too rigid and set in its ways; there may even be a lack of love and of truth. To forgive is also to look into oneself and to see where one should change, where one should also ask for forgiveness and make amends.

To forgive is to recognise once again – after separation – the covenant which binds us together with those we do not get along with well; it is to be open and listening to them once again. It is to give them space in our hearts. That is why it is never easy to forgive. We too must change. We must learn to forgive and forgive and forgive every day, day after day. We need the power of the Holy Spirit in order to open up like that.

A community in which there is truly mutual trust is
a community which is indestructible.

TRUST

The mutual trust at the heart of community is born of each day's forgiveness and acceptance of the frailty and poverty of ourselves and of others. But this trust is not developed overnight. This is why it takes time to form a real community. When people join a community, they always present a certain image of themselves because they want to conform to what the others expect of them. Gradually, they discover that the others love them as they are and trust them. But this trust must stand the test and must always be growing.

It is often after suffering, after very great trials, tensions and the proof of fidelity that trust grows. A community in which there is truly mutual trust is a community which is indestructible.

They need something else in order to grow to greater maturity.

LOVING AND LEAVING

Belonging is for becoming. A young man or woman leaves the family because it has become stifling; they need something else in order to grow to greater maturity. So it is with community. It is for becoming and for the growth of personal consciousness. If for some reason it becomes stifling, then the person may have to take the risk of moving on, no matter how painful the separation may be. Community as such is never an end in itself. It is people and love and communion with God that are the goal. But, of course, a separation of this kind comes only after mature discernment and not just because being in community is painful or because there is a new leader we do not like!

NOURISHMENT

'Give us this day our daily bread'

In a community people are called to co-operate together.

THE POWER OF COMMUNION

In a community, people are called to co-operate together. Work has to be done; food must be bought or cultivated and meals prepared; dishes must be washed and floors cleaned. There has to be clear organisation and discipline in a community; otherwise there will be chaos and terrible inefficiency.

In community, collaboration must find its source in communion. It is because people care for each other and feel called to be with each other, walking towards the same goals, that they co-operate together. Co-operation without communion quickly becomes like a work camp or factory, where unity comes from an exterior reality. And there will be many tensions and strife.

Communion is based on some common inner experience of love; it is the recognition of being one body, one people, called by God to be a source of love and peace. Its fulfilment is more in silence than in words, more in celebration than in work. It is an experience of openness and trust that flows from what is innermost in a person; it is a gift of the Holy Spirit.

Community is above all a place of communion. For this reason it is necessary to give priority in daily life to those realities, symbols, meetings and celebrations that will encourage a consciousness of communion. When a community is just a place of work, it is in danger of dying.

Meals are daily celebrations where we meet each other around the same table to be nourished and share in joy.

MEALS

Meals are daily celebrations where we meet each other around the same table to be nourished and share in joy. They are a particular delight for the body and the senses. So we shouldn't bolt our food under the pretext of having more important or more spiritual things to do than sit at a table. A meal is an important community event which has to be well prepared and fully lived. It is a time when the joy of eating and drinking well merge with the joy of meeting – a marvellous human moment. Human beings don't eat like animals, all in their own corner. Friendship and love make the activity human.

During the course of a meal, each person has to have the chance to meet all the others. Even the simple gesture of passing the potatoes is a natural moment of communication which can bring people out of their isolation. They cannot remain behind the barriers of their depression when they have to ask for the salt. The need for food encourages communication.

It is absolutely essential for us to have moments alone to pray and meet God in silence and quietness.

SOLITUDE AND PRAYER

When we live in community, and everyday life is busy and difficult, it is absolutely essential for us to have moments alone to pray and meet God in silence and quietness. Otherwise, our activity motor will become overheated and whizz around like a chicken without a head.

Do not be afraid that your momentary withdrawal will be detrimental to the community; and do not be afraid that an increase in your personal love for God will in any way diminish your love for your neighbour. On the contrary it will enrich it.

As long as our deepest motivation is not clear to us,
we will remain as weathercocks.

NOURISHMENT FOR GROWTH

We are so deeply divided that we will reflect equally an environment which tends towards the light and concern for others, and one which scorns these values and encourages the desires for power and pleasure. As long as our deepest motivation is not clear to us and as long as we have not chosen the people and the place of our growth in its light, we will remain weak and inconsistent, as changeable as weathercocks.

A community reflects the people who make it up. It has energy founded on hope, but there is also weariness, a search for security and a fear of evolving toward maturity of love and responsibility; it often reflects our fear of dying to our personal instincts.

To grow on the journey toward wholeness and a greater radiance of justice and truth, people, like a community itself, need real nourishment. Without it, the energies of hope will waste away. Instead, there will be desire for pleasure and comfort, or a depressed weariness, or aggression, or a legalistic and bureaucratic approach.

It is never easy to find the harmony between rest,
relaxation and nourishment on one hand,
and generosity and availability on the other.

LOOKING AFTER OURSELVES

I often hear talk of people committed to social action or in communities who are 'burned-out'. These people have been too generous; they have thrown themselves into activity which has finally destroyed them emotionally. They have not known how to relax and to be refreshed. Those in responsibility must teach such people the discipline of physical rest and relaxation, and the need for spiritual nourishment and for fixing clear priorities. They must also set an example.

Rest is one of the most important personal resources, and it has a whole discipline of its own. Sometimes, when we are over-tired, we tend to flit about, doing nothing and spending long hours talking into the night when we would do better to get more sleep. We all have to find our individual rhythm of relaxation and rest.

It is never easy to find the harmony between rest, relaxation and nourishment on one hand, and generosity and availability on the other. Only the Holy Spirit can teach us to love ourselves sufficiently to be able to give our lives as totally as possible. If we are not well, in good shape, joyful and nourished, we will not give life to others; instead, we shall communicate sadness and emptiness.

Daily life is only nourishing when we have discovered
the wisdom of the present moment.

THE PLEASURE OF GIVING ... THE JOY OF RECEIVING

T he essential nourishment is fidelity to the thousand and one small demands of each day, the effort to love and forgive 'the enemy' and to welcome and accept community structures, with all this brings by way of co-operation with authority. It is fidelity in listening to the poor of the community, in accepting a simple and unheroic life. It is fidelity in directing personal projects towards the good of the community and its poorest members and in renouncing purely personal prestige.

Daily life is only nourishing when we have discovered the wisdom of the present moment and the presence of God in small things. It is only nourishing when we have given up fighting reality and accept it, discovering the message and gift of the moment. If we see housework or cooking simply as chores which have to be got through, we will get tired and irritable; we will not be able to see the beauty around us. But if we discover that we live with God and our brothers and sisters through what has to be done in the present moment, we become peaceful.

To be continually present to others, and not only present but nourishing, demands a discipline of body and spirit.

COMMITMENT

*I*t is easy to be generous for a few months or even years. But to be continually present to others, and not only present but nourishing, to keep going in a fidelity which is reborn each morning, demands a discipline of body and spirit. We need a disciplined spiritual and intellectual nourishment.

EVERYDAY LIFE

Being unique within a community

I have always wanted to write a book called
'The Right to be a Rotter'.

BEING ONESELF

I have always wanted to write a book called 'The Right to be a Rotter'. A fairer title is perhaps 'The Right to be Oneself'. One of the great difficulties of community life is that we sometimes force people to be what they are not: we stick an ideal image on them to which they are obliged to conform. We then expect too much of them and are quick to judge or to label. If they don't manage to live up to this image or ideal, then they become afraid they won't be loved or that they will disappoint others. So they feel obliged to hide behind a mask.

Community life brings a painful revelation of our limitations, weaknesses and darkness; the unexpected discovery of the monsters within us is hard to accept. The immediate reaction is to try to destroy the monsters, or to hide them away again, pretending that they don't exist. Or else we try to flee from community life and relationships with others, or to assume that the monsters are theirs not ours. It is the others who are guilty, not us.

It may not be very easy at first. But gradually we discover
what a richness it is to live with such a diversity of people,
and such diversity of gifts.

A DIVERSITY OF GIFTS

a community is like an orchestra: each instrument is beautiful when it plays alone, but when they all play together, each given its own weight in turn, the result is even more beautiful. A community is like a garden full of flowers, shrubs and trees. Each helps to give life to the other. Together, they bear witness to the beauty of God, creator and gardener-extraordinary.

Community brings together people of very different temperaments. Some are organised, quick, precise and efficient; they tend to be defensive and legalistic. Others are open, flexible and love personal contact; they are less efficient – to say the least! Others again are extrovert, optimistic, and even a bit exalted. God calls all these opposites together to create the wealth of the community. It may not be very easy at first. But gradually we discover what a richness it is to live with such a diversity of people, and such diversity of gifts. We discover that difference is not a threat but a treasure, or that 'variety is evidence of life: cold conformity presages death'.

Each person has a gift to use for the good and growth of all.

INDIVIDUAL GIFTS

The gift is not necessarily linked to a function. It may be the quality of love which gives life to a function; it may be a quality of love which has nothing to do with any function. There are people who have the gift of being able to sense immediately, and even to live, the sufferings of others – that is the gift of compassion. There are others who know when something is going wrong and can pinpoint the cause – that is the gift of discernment. There are others who have the gift of light – they see clearly what is of fundamental concern to the community. Others have the gift of creating an atmosphere which brings joy, relaxation and individual growth. Others again have the gift of discerning what people need and of supporting them. Others have the gift of welcome. Each person has a gift to use for the good and growth of all.

It means wanting others to fulfil themselves, according to God's plan and in service to other people. It means wanting them to be faithful to their own calling, free to love in all the dimensions of their being.

82

THE GIFT OF ONESELF

a community is only truly a body when the majority of its members is making the transition from 'the community for myself' to 'myself for the community', when each person's heart is opening to all the others, without any exception. This is the movement from egoism to love, from death to resurrection; it is the Easter, a passage, the Passover of the Lord. It is also the passing from a land of slavery to a promised land, the land of inner freedom.

Love is neither sentimental nor a passing emotion. It is the recognition of a covenant, of a mutual belonging. It is listening to others, being concerned for them and feeling empathy with them. It is to see their beauty and to reveal it to them. It means answering their call and their deepest needs. It means feeling and suffering with them – weeping when they weep, rejoicing when they rejoice.

And if love means moving towards each other, it also and above all means moving together in the same direction, hoping and wishing for the same things. Love means sharing the same vision and the same ideal. So it means wanting others to fulfil themselves, according to God's plan and in service to other people. It means wanting them to be faithful to their own calling, free to love in all the dimensions of their being.

There we have the two poles of community: a sense of belonging to each other and desire that each of us goes further in our own gift to God and to others, a desire for more light in us, and a deeper truth and peace.

There are always those who are resistant to change; they refuse to move on; they would like things to stay as they have always been.

OFFERING, GIVING, NOURISHING

Using our gifts is building community. If we are not faithful to our gifts, we are harming the community and each of its members as well. So it is important that all members know what their gifts are, use them and take responsibility for developing them; it is important that the gift of each member is recognised and that each is accountable to the others for the use to which this gift is put. We all need each other's gifts; we must encourage their growth and our fidelity to them. Everyone will find their place in community according to their gift. They will become not only useful but unique and necessary to the others. And so rivalry and jealousy will evaporate.

Envy is one of the plagues that destroys community.

ENVY

Envy is one of the plagues that destroys community. It comes from people's ignorance of, or lack of belief in, their own gifts. If we were confident in our own gift, we would not envy that of others.

Community is the safe place where all of us feel free to be ourselves and have the confidence to say everything we live and think.

EXPRESS YOURSELF

Community is the safe place where all of us feel free to be ourselves and have the confidence to say everything we live and think. Not all communities will get to this point, it's true. But this is the direction in which they should be going. As long as some people are afraid of expressing themselves, for fear of being judged or thought stupid, or of being rejected, there is still a long way to go. There should be a quality of listening at the heart of the community which tenderly respects everything that is the most beautiful and true in each other.

Self-expression does not mean simply giving vent to all our frustrations and angers at what is going badly – though sometimes it is good to bring these out. It also means sharing our deep motivation and what we are living. It is often a way of using our gift to nurture others and help them grow.

The thousand and one small things that have to be done each day, the cycle of dirtying and cleaning, were given by God to enable us to communicate through matter.

EVERYDAY LIVING

One of the signs that a community is alive can be found in material things. Cleanliness, furnishings, the way flowers are arranged and meals prepared, are among the things which reflect the quality of people's hearts. Some people may find material chores irksome; they would prefer to use their time to talk and be with others. They haven't yet realised that the thousand and one small things that have to be done each day, the cycle of dirtying and cleaning, were given by God to enable us to communicate through matter. Cooking and washing floors can become a way of showing our love for others. If we see the humblest task in this light, everything can become communion and so celebration – because it is celebration to be able to give.

It is important too to recognise the humble and material gifts that others bring and to thank them for them. Recognition of the gifts of others is essential in community. All it takes is a smile and two small words – 'Thank you'. When we put love into what we do, it becomes beautiful, and so do the results. There is a lack of love in a dirty or untidy community. But the greatest beauty is in simplicity and lack of affectation, where everything is oriented towards a meeting of people among themselves and with God.

We need to refind the gift of youth and peaceful wisdom of age.

YOUNG AND OLD, LIVING TOGETHER

*I*t is always good when a community has a wide spread of ages, from the very young to the very old. The complementarity, as in a family, brings peace. When everyone is the same age, it can be exciting for a time, but weariness soon sets in. We need to refind the gift of youth and the peaceful wisdom of age.

Leaders need to animate the community, so that it continues
to be alive and the eyes of all are fixed on essential goals.

TAKING CARE OF THE COMMUNITY

*T*he people who carry responsibility in a community have received a mission which has been bestowed on them either by the community which elected them, or by a superior (or some other external authority) who has appointed them and to whom they are accountable. But the mission is always received from God.

Leaders of communities need to organise the community so that each member is in the right place and things work smoothly. They need to animate it, so that it continues to be alive and the eyes of all are fixed on the essential goals. They need to love each person and be concerned about their growth. Members can sense very quickly if those with responsibility in the community love and trust them and want to help them grow, or if they are there just to prove their authority, impose the rules and their own vision, or else are seeking to please.

To lead is to judge situations and make wise decisions.

FEELING RESPONSIBLE FOR OTHERS

*T*o lead is to judge situations and make wise decisions. And judgement is always in respect to certain criteria; these criteria are the goal or objectives of the community.

To exercise authority is to feel truly responsible for others and their growth, knowing too that the 'others' are not their property, are not objects but people with hearts in whom resides the light of God, and who are called to grow to the freedom of truth and love. The greatest danger for someone in authority is to manipulate people and to control them for his or her own goals and need for power.

The essential, for all people with authority, is that they are servants before they are bosses. People who assume responsibility to prove something, because they tend to be dominating and controlling, because they need to see themselves at the top or because they are looking for privileges and prestige, will always exercise their responsibility badly. They must first want to be servants.

MISSION

Being open and welcoming
to others and to the world

If we do not have the spiritual nourishment we need, we will perhaps be polite and obedient, but we will not love.

THE RISK OF CLOSING IN UPON OURSELVES

C ommunity life demands that we constantly go beyond our own resources. If we do not have the spiritual nourishment we need, we will close in on ourselves and on our own comfort and security, or throw ourselves into work as an escape. We will throw up walls around our sensitivity; we will perhaps be polite and obedient, but we will not love.

And when you do not love, there is no hope and no joy. It is terrible to see people living sadly in community, without love. To live with *gratuité*, we have to be constantly nourished.

Communities are truly communities when they are open to others, when they remain vulnerable and humble; when the members are growing in love, in compassion and in humility. Communities cease to be such when members close in upon themselves with the certitude that they alone have wisdom and truth and expect everyone to be like them and learn from them.

Their love, their emotional stability, their children,
bring so much to the weaker people – and to us all.

COMMUNITY AND FAMILY

*I*n many ways communities are like families. But there are clear distinctions. To start a family, two people must choose each other and promise fidelity. It is the fidelity and love of these two people which bring peace, health and growth to the children who are born of their love. When we come into community, we do not promise to be faithful to one person. The parental roles – those of the people at the head of the community – change according to the constitution, and we do not commit ourselves to live always with the same people. It can be wonderful for a community when there are families in it; and it can be wonderful for families to be in community. But it must be clear that a family in itself is a little community. Its own dynamic and originality must be respected. The family must be enabled to forge its own unity. A couple is not the same as two single people living together; it is two people who have become one.

It is a great richness to have married people at l'Arche. Most of them cannot live in a house with handicapped people, because they need their own place. And because a family is itself a community, it must never be sacrificed to the larger community. But even though families cannot live all the time with handicapped people, their presence in the community is important. Their love, their emotional stability, their children, bring so much to the weaker people – and to us all.

It is always a risk to welcome anyone and particularly the stranger.

WELCOMING WITH DISCERNMENT

*I*t is always a risk to welcome anyone and particularly the stranger. It is always disturbing. But didn't Jesus come precisely to disturb our routines, comforts, and apathy? We need constant challenge if we are not to become dependent on security and comfort, if we are to continue to progress from the slavery of sin and egoism towards the promised land of liberation.

To welcome means listening a great deal to people and then discerning the truth with them. A community cannot accept as a resident every single person that knocks at the door. In order to welcome there must be a peaceful space in the hearts of those welcoming and a peaceful space in the community for the person to find a place of rest and growth. If that peaceful space is lacking then it is better not to welcome.

At the same time, the people welcomed must try to accept the community as it is, with the space that is offered, be willing to abide by the spirit, traditions and rules of the community, and desire also to grow and to evolve. If the newcomer only wants to change the community and get everything they can out of it, without any modification on their part, there can be no true welcome.

There are times when it is important to knock down
the walls of a community.

OPEN TO THE WORLD

The more a community deepens and grows, the more integrated it must be in the neighbourhood. When it begins, a community is contained within the four walls of its house. But gradually it opens up to neighbours and friends. Some communities begin to panic when they feel that their neighbours are becoming committed to them; they are frightened of losing their identity, of losing control. But isn't this what true expansion means? There are times when it is important to knock down the walls of a community. This demands that each person respect the other's commitment and that their rights and responsibilities are clearly explained. Each person must become responsible for the others in a specific way. Each must freely bring something to the others and true bonds must be woven. This is how a small community can gradually become the yeast in the dough, a place of unity for all and between all.

A community must always remember that it is a sign and witness to all humankind. Its members must be faithful to each other if they are to grow. But they must also be faithful as a sign and source of hope for all humankind.

One of the risks that God will always ask of a community
is that it welcomes visitors, especially the poorest people,
the ones who disturb us.

WELCOMING THE STRANGER

One of the risks that God will always ask of a community is that it welcomes visitors, especially the poorest people, the ones who disturb us. Very often God brings a particular message to the community through an unexpected guest, letter or telephone call.

The day the community starts to turn away visitors and the unexpected, the day it calls a halt, is the day it is in danger of shutting itself off from the action of God. Did not Jesus say: 'I was the stranger and you welcomed me'? Staying open to Providence demands a very great availability.

The poor are a source of life and not just objects of our charity.

LISTENING TO THE POOR

Communities which start by serving the poor must gradually discover the gifts brought by those they serve. The communities start in generosity; they must grow in the ability to listen. In the end, the most important thing is not to do things for people who are poor and in distress, but to enter into relationship with them, to be with them and help them find confidence in themselves and discover their own gifts. It isn't a question of arriving in a slum with the money to build a dispensary and a school. It is more a question of spending time with the people who live in the slum to help them discover their own needs and then together building what they want. Perhaps these buildings won't be as beautiful. But they will be more used and loved, because they will belong to everyone and not just to a foreigner who means well. It will take a long time. But all service which is really human takes time. The promise of Jesus is to help us discover that the poor are a source of life and not just objects of our charity. If we are close to them, we will be renewed in love and in faith.

When a community lets itself be guided in its growth by the cry of the poor and their needs, it will walk in the desert and it will be insecure. But it is assured of the promised land – not the one of security, but the one of peace and love. And it will be a community which is always alive.

Community enables us to welcome and help people in a way we couldn't as individuals.

THE VOCATION OF WELCOMING

One of the marvellous things about community is that it enables us to welcome and help people in a way we couldn't as individuals. When we pool our strength and share the work and responsibility, we can welcome many more people, even those in deep distress, and perhaps help them find self-confidence and inner healing.

To welcome is one of the signs of true human and Christian maturity. It is not only to open one's door and one's home to someone. It is to give space to someone in one's heart, space for that person to be and to grow; space where the person knows that he or she is accepted just as they are, with their wounds and their gifts. That implies the existence of a quiet and peaceful place in the heart where people can find a resting place. If the heart is not peaceful, it cannot welcome.

But to be able to welcome means that our inner person and freedom have been strengthened; we are no longer a person living in fear and insecurity, unclear about who we are and what is our mission. It takes time for this inner person to grow. It takes many painful meetings, many times when we have been wrong and have asked for forgiveness, much grace from God and much love from loving friends. To become humble and open, we have to live through many humiliations.

Revealing to others their fundamental beauty, value and importance in the universe, transmitting to people a new inner freedom and hope.

YOU ARE VALUED

Mission is revealing to others their fundamental beauty, value and importance in the universe, their capacity to love, to grow and to do beautiful things and to meet God. Mission is transmitting to people a new inner freedom and hope; it is unlocking the doors of their being so that new energies can flow; it is taking away from their shoulders the terrible yoke of fear and guilt. To give life to people is to reveal to them that they are loved just as they are by God, with the mixture of good and evil, light and darkness that is in them: that the stone in front of their tomb in which all the dirt of their lives has been hidden, can be rolled away. They are forgiven. They can live in freedom.

The mission of a community is to give life to others, that is to say, to transmit new hope and new meaning to them.

GIVING LIFE

The mission of a community is to give life to others, that is to say, to transmit new hope and new meaning to them.

When Jesus sent his disciples out on mission, he told them to be poor, to take nothing with them. And he told them to do things that were impossible for them to do all by themselves. So it is for all missions. Communities and their members are called to be poor and to do impossible things, such as to build community and to bring healing, reconciliation, forgiveness and wholeness to people. Mission is to bring the life of God to others, and this can only be done if communities and people are poor and humble, letting the life of God flow through them. Mission implies this double poverty, but also trust in the call and the power of God manifested through poverty, littleness and humility.

Celebration is an essential element in community life.

CELEBRATION!

Celebration expresses the true meaning of community in a concrete and tangible way. So it is an essential element in community life. Celebration sweeps away the irritations of daily life; we forget our little quarrels. The aspect of ecstasy in a celebration unites our hearts; a current of life goes through us all. Celebration is a moment of wonder when the joy of the body and senses are linked to the joy of the spirit. It unites everything that is most human and most divine in community life. The liturgy of the celebration – which brings together music, dance, song, light and the fruit and flowers of the earth – brings us into communion with God and each other, through prayer, thanksgiving and good food. (And the celebratory meal is important!) The harder and more irksome our daily life, the more our hearts need these moments of celebration and wonder. We need times when we all come together to give thanks, sing, dance and enjoy special meals. Each community, like each people, needs its festival liturgy.

At the heart of celebration, there are the poor. If the least significant is excluded it is no longer a celebration. We have to find dances and games in which the children, the old people, and the weak can join equally. A celebration must always be a festival of the poor, and with the poor, not for the poor.

Our journey together, our pilgrimage, is worthwhile. This is hope.

LET'S GO!

Community life is there to help us, not to flee from our deep wound, but to remain with the reality of love. It is there to help us believe that our illusions and egoism will be gradually healed if we become nourishment for others. We are in community for each other so that all of us can grow and uncover our wound before the infinite, so that Jesus can manifest himself through it.

Community is there not for itself, but for others – the poor, the Church and society. It is essentially mission. It has a message of hope to offer and a love to communicate, especially to those who are poor and in distress. So community has a political aspect.

So community life takes on a wider meaning. It is lived not only among its own members, but in the larger community of its neighbourhood, with the poor, and with all those who want to share its hope. So it becomes a place of reconciliation and forgiveness, where each person feels carried by the others and carries them. It is a place of friendship among those who know that they are weak but know too that they are loved and forgiven. Thus community is a place of celebration.

Our journey together, our pilgrimage, is worthwhile. This is hope.

Nem (Houses Co-ordinator) and Milly (core member)

L'ARCHE

The strength of our relationships makes us different
Building community with people with learning disabilities

L'Arche Communities provide relationships and activities that support the whole person, including their emotional and spiritual needs. L'Arche Communities ensure people are not isolated and lonely, but instead lead happy and fulfilling lives.

Laura (core member) and Amy (friend of the community, former assistant)

Crispin (core member) and Kevin (Community Leader)

L'Arche believes in a world where everybody belongs and, as such, supports each individual so that they can grow and shape their own unique role in the world.

Emma (core member) and Megan (assistant)

Laura (core member) and Kevin (Community Leader)

There are 12 L'Arche Communities and projects in the UK that support nearly 300 people with learning disabilities. These are networks of people across towns and cities who live, work and celebrate life together in community.

What makes L'Arche Special?

- L'Arche Communities are relationship focused

- L'Arche Communities are places of belonging; where people can build lasting connections, friendships and relationships.

- L'Arche Communities support people to draw on the resources of their own spiritual life.

- L'Arche is international. There are Communities in more than 35 countries and assistants come from nearly every continent. L'Arche opens up the opportunity to travel and build engagement across the world.

'Every person needs to know they are a source of joy: every person needs to be celebrated.' Jean Vanier, founder of L'Arche and winner of the 2015 Templeton Prize.

There are L'Arche Communities in Bognor, Brecon, Edinburgh, Highland, Ipswich, Kent, Liverpool, Manchester and Preston and projects in Flintshire and Nottingham.

www.larche.org.uk

Photographs are of L'Arche Manchester © L'Arche/Jarek Maciejowski